Breaking Free

Changing Your Life Forever

Robb D. Thompson

Unless otherwise indicated, all Scripture quotations are taken from the Holy Bible: New King James Version, copyright © 1982 by Thomas Nelson, Inc. All rights reserved.

Scripture quotations marked NIV are taken from The Holy Bible: New International Version®. NIV®. Copyright © 1973, 1978, 1984 by International Bible Society. Used by permission of Zondervan Publishing House. All rights reserved.

Scripture quotations marked NLT are taken from The Holy Bible: New Living Translation. Copyright © 1996 by Tyndale Charitable Trust. All rights reserved.

Scripture quotations marked The Message are taken from The Message New Testament With Psalms and Proverbs. Copyright © 1993, 1994, 1995 by Eugene H. Peterson. Published by NavPress Publishing Group. All rights reserved.

Scriptures marked as WE are taken from The Bible in Worldwide English New Testament. Copyright © 1996 by SOON Educational Publications. Used by permission.

Breaking Free: Changing Your Life Forever
ISBN 1-889723-63-0

Copyright © 2005 by Robb Thompson
Family Harvest Church
18500 92nd Ave.
Tinley Park, Illinois 60487

Collaborative Development: Karen Jahn, Dr. Dennis D. Sempebwa
Editing: Karen Jahn
Design: Amanda Fico

Printed in Canada.
All rights reserved under International Copyright Law.
Contents and/or cover may not be reproduced in whole or in part in any form without the express written consent of the Publisher.

CONTENTS

1
Identifying the Voices..........................Pg 9

2
The Keys of the Kingdom.................Pg 15

3
Trust the Book, Not Your Brain........Pg 21

4
Get the Picture....................................Pg 29

5
What Are You Looking At?................Pg 41

6
Your Future is in Your Mouth...........Pg 47

7
Be Responsive, Not Reactive.............Pg 59

Preface

Each and every one of us face moments of mental chaos that cause us to stop in our tracks. A toxic thought invades, and for a moment, we freeze. We hope that it will go away. We even pray for it to go away—but still no relief. What, then, can we do?

Already a critical tool used to help people walk free, *Breaking Free* shows you how to take control of your life and live as God intended for you to live. You will learn:

- How To Identify God's Voice.
- The Necessary Keys To Access The Promises Of God.
- The Importance Of Trusting God's Book And Not Your Emotions.
- How To Paint The Right Mental Picture Of Yourself.

And much more…

If you have a desire—or maybe a passion—for walking victoriously and helping others do the same, Robb Thompson will help you discover the principles that will bring your desire to pass. Let *Breaking Free* give you a fresh start and help you set your life on the path of FREEDOM!

Chapter 1

Identifying The Voices

Each and every one of us face moments of mental chaos that cause us to stop in our tracks. A toxic thought invades our mind, and for a moment we freeze. We hope it will go away. We even pray for it to go away—but still no relief. What can we do?

There isn't a person alive who can avoid these mental battles. If you are saying that you have never had renegade thoughts race through your mind, then the only person that you are fooling, right now, is yourself. And the only one who is happy about your cover up is the one who gave you the destructive thoughts to begin with. Your enemy realizes that the fear of embarrassment could keep you from admitting your struggle, and therefore, keep you from your deliverance.

These thoughts begin to bother you and, eventually, to torment you. You can't seem to get free. From the time you wake up until you lay your head down at night (and into the wee hours of the night), the taxing inner monologue seems to suck you into its vortex of fear. People call it a bad day. Then you have a string of consecutive bad days, and it's called depression.

> SOUND THOUGHTS ARE RUDDERS ON THE SHIP WHICH GUIDE US THROUGH THE STORMS OF LIFE.

How can you overcome the negative thoughts that bombard your mind? How can you live the life that God has for you? What can you do to get a grip on your thinking and transform your life?

The first thing you must realize is that two things ***did not*** get saved when you did: *your body* and *your mind.* These two arenas are really where all problems have been birthed. They both have loud voices, and they are both battling for the control of your heart. Your body must be subdued, and your mind must be renewed.

Let's examine these concepts further.

What happened to us the moment that we actually received Jesus Christ as the Lord of our lives? What happened to us when we were born again? Jesus told Nicodemus that unless a person was born again, he could not see the Kingdom of Heaven. When Nicodemus expressed surprise and confusion at this remark, Jesus explained with these words, *"The truth is, no one can enter the Kingdom of God without being born of water and the Spirit. Humans can reproduce only human life, but the Holy Spirit gives new life from heaven. So don't be surprised at my statement that you must be born again"* (John 3:5-7, *NLT*). Jesus made a definite distinction between the flesh and the spirit. He made it very clear that a "born again" experience redeems the *spirit* of a man, not his flesh.

Your body did not get saved when you did. Have you noticed that? You were redeemed, but your body was not. Your outward man is perishing. Every day, death tries to creep into your flesh. 2 Corinthians 4:16 (*NLT*) says, *"…Though our bodies are dying, our spirits are being renewed every day."*

Because your body is continually trying to

protect itself from this incessant progression of decay, it demands constant attention. Like a spoiled toddler throwing a temper tantrum, it insists on being heard. As a matter of fact, your body has a voice; it's called feelings and emotions. Your flesh will use this "voice," in an attempt to distract you from the very thing that God desires for you to believe—His Word.

You and your body are two different entities. That's why the Apostle Paul said, *"...I beat my body and I make it my slave..."* (1 Corinthians 9:27, *NIV*). Now, that's an odd thing to say. Why did he say that? Because, as you have probably discovered, your body has a mind of its own; it still has shocking desires. Your body does not want to do what *you* want to do. In Romans 7, Paul spoke of this constant struggle:

> **I don't understand myself at all, for I really want to do what is right, but I don't do it. Instead, I do the very thing I hate. I know perfectly well that what I am doing is wrong, and my bad conscience shows that I agree that the law is good.**
>
> ***Romans 7:15-16 (NLT)***

When I want to do good, I don't. And when I try not to do wrong, I do it anyway. But if I am doing

what I don't want to do, I am not really the one doing it; the sin within me is doing it.

Romans 7:19-20 (NLT)

Some people are possessed by demons before they get saved. When they come to Christ, those demons are cast out; they can't stay where God has moved in! But whether or not we have demons when we come to the Lord, we *all* have a flesh.

Your flesh must be crucified daily, because it hates you. Paul tells us in Romans 8:6-8 (*Worldwide English New Testament*), that your flesh will do everything in its power to sabotage your spiritual walk with God:

If you keep your mind on the things your bodies want to do, you will die. But if you keep your mind on the things the Spirit wants, you will live and have peace. People who think about the things of this life are God's enemies. They do not obey God's law. They cannot obey it. People who do what their bodies want cannot please God.

YOU CAN'T CRUCIFY A DEMON, AND YOU CAN'T CAST OUT YOUR FLESH.

People make this mistake quite often. A demon has to be cast out. But, again, *you cannot cast out your flesh; it must be crucified.*

The other thing that did not get saved, when you did, is your mind. Your mind has a voice that's even louder than your body's. Your mind thinks all sorts of wild and crazy things, at all hours of the day and night! You find yourself wondering, "Where in the world did *that* come from?"

That way of thinking may be a generational curse passed down from your great, great, great grandfather, whom you may have never met; but you can rest assured that directly or indirectly, every destructive thought comes from hell itself. We must come to grips with the fact that the majority of thoughts that go through our minds *do not* have God as their source.

That's the reason that God wants us continually programming ourselves with His Words. He tells us that if we continually keep our minds fixed on the things that *He* has spoken, we won't have to be oppressed by the lying voices that try to lure us every day. Joshua 1:8 says, *"This Book of the Law shall not depart from your mouth, but you shall meditate in it day and night, that you may observe to do according to all that is written in it. For then you will make your way prosperous, and then you will have good success."*

Chapter 2

The Keys Of The Kingdom

In Matthew 16:19, Jesus made a fascinating statement. He said, *"And I will give you the keys of the kingdom of heaven..."* Notice the phrase "the keys *of* the kingdom." He did not say "the keys *to* the kingdom." Why is this significant?

I could have the key *to* your house, but that doesn't mean I have the keys *of* your house. It is true that the key *to* your house would get me in the front door; but then I might still find that every door inside your house is locked. I want more than the key *to* your house—I want the keys *of* your house.

In the same way, Jesus wants you to experience more than just getting inside the front door of heaven. He said, "I will give you the keys *of* the kingdom." In other words, "I want you to experience, in this life, every treasure and promise that is hidden inside My Word!"

Access to the precious treasures of God's Word is not given in a casual or haphazard manner. I must apply all that I am to the search! I must continually ask, seek, and knock. I must learn to love God and to esteem His Word *more than anything else in life.*

Ironically, this may be one of your greatest challenges, if you've gone to church your whole life. If you've grown up in the church, you may begin to see the Word of God from a carnal perspective: "Well, this is just church. This is just what we do at church." You may not understand that *your whole life* needs to conform to God's Word.

THE BIBLE IS NOT JUST ANOTHER BOOK; IT IS THE OWNER'S MANUAL FOR LIFE.

Have you been listening to the voices of your unredeemed body or your unrenewed mind? Have you yet to discover the things that have held you back in life? What are these things that seem to stand in the way of your becoming everything you need to be? The choices of today really do matter toward the outcome of tomorrow.

All of life is tied to this reality: *"God is not a man, that He should lie, nor a son of man, that He should repent. Has He said, and will He not do? Or has He spoken, and will He not make it good?"* (Numbers 23:19)

Sometimes the most difficult thing for us to do is to get honest with ourselves. As Christians, we may believe that we're trusting God's Word, and be deeply puzzled and disappointed when failure continues to plague our lives. It is at this point that we may need to ask ourselves, "What do I *really believe*? What kind of outcome am I really expecting, in this situation?"

Here is an example to illustrate how subtly doubt and unbelief can invade our lives:

It's wonderful to just lie on the beach and watch the ocean. The waves are rolling in and rolling out; it's just beautiful. But then, all of a sudden, you see a flag that says, "Dangerous Undertow."

Now, let me explain what happens in many people's lives. In fact, this might be happening to you, without your even realizing it.

Like the ocean waves, everything on the surface looks wonderful. You think, "I'm really rolling here—I'm believing the right things, and I'm doing the right things. Man, I'm telling you, I am really getting after it. God's Word is exactly what I believe, and no matter what, I'm holding on to it."

And yet, you're not experiencing any change—you're not really seeing any fruit from your believing. So then the devil comes and tells you that there is something wrong with you, and that God doesn't love you; and your outside circumstances seem to confirm the devil's lies. Now, what are you to believe?

Here is the issue: Just like the beautiful ocean, you can have the outside of your life looking wonderful—yet on the *inside,* there is turmoil. You are headed in a different direction, and don't even realize it. It's the undertow. *The undertow is what you truly believe.*

You might say, "I believe I'm healed; but I'm still going to take my sick days."

No, wait a minute. The spiritual world does not understand this statement. Could you possibly be sending mixed messages to the angels who stand at attention waiting to perform the Word of God in your life? (*See* Hebrews 1:14) The angels and the demons obey what you *say, out of the abundance of your heart.* They obey the force of the undertow that's coming out of you. In the spirit realm, whatever *we say* is what *they* are going to do—***whatever we say.***

It is out of the abundance of your heart that your mouth speaks (Luke 6:45). Are you pouring a fresh supply of God's Word into your life every day, so that it becomes the abundance of your heart, causing words of victory to come out of your mouth? In Galatians 3:3 (*NLT*), the Apostle Paul explains the futility of trying to live a victorious life in your own natural strength: *"Have you lost your senses? After starting your Christian lives in the Spirit, why are you now trying to become perfect by your own human effort?"*

Beware of religion. Religion is simply man's attempt to please God through his own human efforts. Religion declares that it's OK to:

- Go to church, but don't make your life revolve around God's Word.
- Just fit the Word in when you can—if you can get to it; God understands.

- Believe that you can manage this way, because you "know" what it says on the pages.
- Not be too bothered by the fact that God's Word is not really first place in your life anymore; after all, He still loves you.

Friend, the Word of God is the only thing that will never change. The Word of God is the thing that has the ability to keep you alive.

STOP TRYING TO APPLY THE WORD TO YOUR LIFE, AND BEGIN TO APPLY YOUR LIFE TO THE WORD.

We can't expect to see growth, change, or mind prosperity in our lives if we merely apply a scripture to a situation as it arises (as we would apply a band-aid to a wound.) Because the Word of God is the only constant, unchanging element that we will ever have in our lives, every aspect and detail of our lives must be molded, shaped, and driven by its precepts and principles.

Chapter 3

Trust The Book, Not Your Brain

If you are crying out to God for a real *breakthrough*, you must come to the discovery of these truths:

1. *All of Eternity Rests On This One Point:*

God is not a man, that He should lie, nor a son of man, that He should repent. Has He said, and will He not do? Or has He spoken, and will He not make it good?

Numbers 23:19

2. *All of the Believer's Life is Decided by This Exercise:*

And so, dear brothers and sisters, I plead with you to give your bodies to God. Let them be a living and holy sacrifice—the kind he will accept. When you think of what he has done for you, is this too much to ask? Don't copy the behavior and customs of this world, but let God transform you into a new person by changing the way you think. Then you will know what God wants you to do, and you will know how good and pleasing and perfect his will really is.

Romans 12:1-2 (NLT)

3. *No Other Exercise Can Take the Place of Meditation Upon and the Confession of God's Word.*

Then Jesus said to those Jews who believed Him, "If you abide in My Word, you are My disciples indeed. And you shall know the truth, and the truth shall make you free."

John 8:31-32

Now, I'm talking to you about truly *breaking free*. I am not advocating for you to cry out for a miracle. One of the greatest challenges that exists in the Body of Christ today, is that many of us are way too miracle oriented—we want to live our lives going from miracle to miracle rather than from faith to faith.

Do you know how few people actually get healed at a typical miracle service? There may be 20,000 people at a meeting, and an average of twenty people might get miraculously healed. Take that percentage and put it inside your life, and that's the likelihood of your getting a miracle.

God's desire for the Christian life is not that a believer would live from miracle to miracle. He wants us to progressively mature into new spiritual realms—to live at another dimension and experience daily, consistent growth, excellence, and victory in our lives.

This is why the following principle is so vital:

THE INTAKE OF BIBLE DOCTRINE IS THE MOST IMPORTANT THING TO A BELIEVER'S LIFE.

The consistent intake of the Word of God, on a daily basis, is the only thing that will bring you to the point of accurate truth and mental stability.

Psalm 119:11 tells us, *"Your word I have hidden in my heart, that I might not sin against You."* Once you have hidden the Word of God in your heart, the only assignment your mind has is to bow in unending submission and obedience to that Word. Irish poet William Butler Yeats once wrote, "The only business of the head in the world is to bow a ceaseless obeisance to the heart." But how does one hide the Word in his heart?

God gave us a mouth to overcome our mind! The only thing that can stop the belligerently screaming thoughts that invade your mind is *your mouth*. What you say with your mouth will determine your future. If you succumb to fear and say the negative thoughts, you have just entered into the prayer of agreement with all that despises you. You have given hell permission to bring those destructive circumstances into your life.

However, faith says what God says! Faith speaks of future events with as much confidence as if they have already come to pass. ***Confession of God's Word is the prayer of agreement with God.*** When you declare God's Word, you have just given the spirit realm what it needs to bring that declaration to pass in your life!

Again, beware of the subtle snare of religion. Religion says that if you believe something, that is good enough. Religion says you can just think, rather than speak. The language of religion is "Christian semantics," but it's not where the life of God lives. It has a form of godliness (2 Timothy 3:5), but it denies the power of the spoken Word, and it produces nothing but frustration.

If the Word of God can't change my life and set me free, then don't tell me about it! True Christianity is not semantically expressed. It's about living from a sincere, seeking heart—*from within.* Sincerity will take you much further than legalism. Semantic Christianity will not work in the face of crisis and tragedy. It will merely conform you to the doctrines of men.

Only one factor separates the transformed from the conformed—*action.* If you want to be transformed, you must actively confess the Word! You must put it in your mouth day and night. James 1:21 says that the implanted Word is able to save your soul (keep your mind insulated from mental torment).

Yes, there is a price to pay, in learning to consistently speak the Word of God. But no matter what the cost seems to be, the price will be paid, regardless of whether or not we press in to confessing God's Word.

WE UNDERESTIMATE BOTH THE COST OF OBEDIENCE, AND THE PRICE FOR OUR DISOBEDIENCE.

The price I pay for purity is always on my mind and in my mouth. The price I pay for impurity is seen on my body, in my corrupted mind, and therefore in my future.

Joshua had to pay a price to step into the position God had for him. God told him, "I want My Word *in your mouth* at all times, day and night. I don't want you just *thinking* about me—I want you *talking* about me. I don't want you just *thinking* about My Word—I want you *saying* My Word. Because when you turn your mouth on, you turn those thoughts off!"

There is a protective cover over the Word of God that the non-committed will never be able to crack. Many do not have the resolution to hang in there long enough for God's Word to release its nectar into their lives.

We must understand this truth: The Bible will not give up its nectar to us just because we say we want it. Until we have ceaselessly examined, pondered, mulled over, and orally recited one scripture, day and night, we will not be able to penetrate its protective shell. Without confession of the Word, we will never, ever break its shell and drink its nectar.

At any given moment, you are either confessing the Word or meditating on your problem. And you can be assured that what you are meditating on *will* find its way out of your mouth!

Here is a practical example. Let us assume that you are dealing with the flu, and someone asks, "How are you?" You have two options: you can say you're healed, or you can say you have the flu. So, which are you? Well, the Bible says that you're healed by the stripes of Jesus (1 Peter 2:24).

"Then why am I dealing with these symptoms?"

Because the flu is <u>A</u> truth; but God's Word is <u>*THE*</u> truth. Therefore, we do not look at the things that are seen—we must never look at the runny nose or the scratchy throat—we must fix our gaze upon the stripes of Jesus. With our mouth, we must declare, "Father, I thank You that You sent forth Your Word and it healed me and delivered me from all destruction" (Psalm 107:20). Always keep in mind that this is *not semantics*. It is *THE* truth.

Breaking Free

> **FREEDOM IS
> AN INTERNAL JOURNEY,
> NOT THE ABSENCE OF
> EXTERNAL TURMOIL.**

Any health, growth, or increase in life occurs only through soul prosperity. When we fill our minds with His Word, our souls begin to prosper. Health and prosperity do not happen in the external realm, before first happening in our minds. This is where most well-meaning believers fail. We must begin today to infiltrate our minds with Heaven's thoughts; then and *only then* will we truly be on the path to breaking free.

Chapter 4

Get The Picture

Have you ever noticed that you don't think in words? No, you think in *pictures*. Try this little experiment. Have someone call out the name of an object to you—for instance, "carrot." When they say the name of the object, what do you "see" in your mind? Do you see the *word* "carrot," or do you see a *picture* of a carrot? I have yet to find anyone who mentally sees the word. Our minds think in pictures.

As we have already discussed, our lives will move in the direction of our most dominant thoughts. And since thoughts are pictures, consider this principle:

OUR LIVES WILL ALWAYS MOVE IN THE DIRECTION OF OUR MOST DOMINANT MENTAL IMAGES.

Now, this is an extremely valuable principle to know, if you want to *create* the future you desire, rather than just passively say, "Whatever will be will be." Are you tired of your present life situations? Do you want your life to move in a different direction? Then what you must do is *paint some different mental images!*

You may even have some pertinent information about what you should do to see your life improve. But as you have probably discovered, information alone will not actually change your life. That *information* must become *revelation*, if you want to see the direction of your life begin to change. The principles of change must become real to you. Only when they become *real* to you will they transform your life.

MEDITATION IS THE AVENUE THROUGH WHICH INFORMATION BECOMES REVELATION.

Meditation is not some Eastern religious practice. Meditation simply means to ponder or to go over and over something in your mind, *until it paints a picture.* When the details of that picture are crystal clear, in your mind's eye, *it will begin to change your life.* That mental picture will affect your attitude, your words, your choices, your decision-making processes, your reasoning skills, and your relationships. Everything about your life will begin to move in the direction of your inner image. And I am certain, the day will come when the outside of your life will match the picture that you've been carrying on the inside.

God created you in such a way that the visible circumstances of your life will manifest and replicate the picture that is on the inside of you.

YOUR FUTURE PROSPERITY LIES IN THE PRESENT CONFINES OF YOUR MIND.

This is true for any area of your life, including your finances. Whatever you predominantly give your thoughts to will create your future. As God's children, it is His desire that we give our thoughts predominantly to Him and to His Word, so that our futures can be abundantly prospered.

The creative power of meditation was revealed to Joshua at a time when he was feeling quite fearful and overwhelmed. His mentor, Moses, had just died. Joshua had been appointed by God to take Moses' place and step into the position of leading the Israelites into the Promised Land. The responsibility was daunting, and he really needed some major reassurance.

So God told Joshua, "Now look, I know you're afraid. I know you want to quit. I know you're not sure if you can lead these people. But, Joshua, you can do this—and now I'm going to tell you how.

"This is what you do," He said. "You put My

Word in front of your eyes, in your thoughts, and in your mouth—meditate on it day and night. Stay inside there long enough for My Word to paint you a picture. Once you can see yourself in that picture, you will succeed and prosper" (author's paraphrase of Joshua 1:8).

Let's read this passage, found in Joshua 1:7-9:

Only be strong and very courageous, that you may observe to do according to all the law which Moses My servant commanded you; do not turn from it to the right hand or to the left, that you may prosper wherever you go.

This Book of the Law shall not depart from your mouth, but you shall meditate in it day and night, *that you may observe to do* according to all that is written in it. For then you will make your way prosperous, and then you will have good success.

Have I not commanded you? Be strong and of good courage; do not be afraid, nor be dismayed, for the LORD your God is with you wherever you go.

You see, God can call us to do something, but without a clear mental picture, we cannot complete it.

Now, God can't just give you a picture. *You* have to paint the picture. God may give you a vision, but

Habakkuk 2:3 says, *"For the vision is yet for an appointed time…"*—and when that time arrives, you need to be prepared.

What do you do to prepare? You get a picture. How do you get a picture? ***By meditating on the Word.***

When I discovered this secret, I knew I could laugh at the days to come (*See* Job 5:22, Proverbs 31:25, *NLT*). Why? Because I already have the picture! Psalm 112:7 (*NLT*) says, *"They do not fear bad news; they confidently trust the Lord to care for them."* I can laugh because I already know the outcome. It doesn't really matter to me how long it takes, because I know the answer already. Your life will change when you are able to focus more on the answers than on the problems.

It is only when the information on the pages of God's Word becomes *real* that it will change your life. As you continually look into the Word of God for your answers to every situation of life, the Word will paint a picture for you. That "Word picture" will change the way you think. It will change the way you live. It will change everything about you. And there is no other way for that inner transformation to take place.

David reiterates the importance of meditation, in the following Psalms:

> **Oh, how I love Your law! It is my meditation all the day.**
>
> ***Psalm 119:97***

> **But his delight is in the law of the LORD,**
> **And in His law he meditates day and night.**
> **He shall be like a tree**
> **Planted by the rivers of water,**
> **That brings forth its fruit in its season,**
> **Whose leaf also shall not wither;**
> **And whatever he does shall prosper.**
>
> ***Psalm 1:2-3***

Let's look at *The Message* version of Psalm 1:1-3:

> **How well God must like you—you don't hang out at Sin Saloon, you don't slink along Dead-End Road, you don't go to Smart-Mouth College.**
>
> **Instead you thrill to God's Word, you chew on Scripture day and night.**
>
> **You're a tree replanted in Eden, bearing fresh fruit every month, never dropping a leaf, always in blossom.**

Remember, there is a covering over the scripture that is only cracked open by those who are most committed to *continual* pursuit. As I continually meditate upon what God has said—as I continually think about it and meditate on it, and actually muse over this one issue all day, all night, all day, all night—*it gives me a picture. Until I get a picture, I simply cannot break free.*

God wants us to stay inside of His Word long enough for it to create snapshots of success within our hearts and minds. These images are the starting points of your deliverance. When you begin to *see* what God has for you, you will begin to *act* in such a way that you'll break free from the mental pressures and the mistakes of your past.

Joshua understood how crucial it was to get the picture. Exodus 33:11 tells us:

So the LORD spoke to Moses face to face, as a man speaks to his friend. And he would return to the camp, but his servant Joshua the son of Nun, a young man, did not depart from the tabernacle.

Why did Joshua stay in the tent of meeting long after Moses had left? *Because he needed a picture.* The presence of God is what brings a picture.

You've got to seek out your own face-to-face encounters with God. You've got to soak yourself in His presence and in His precepts. You've got to pray in the Spirit—not just in your understanding, but also in the Spirit. This brings you a picture, because you're praying mysteries (1 Corinthians 14:2). You're bringing forth mysteries, just as a woman brings forth a child. You birth the plans and purposes of heaven into your every day life.

Those purposes have to be prayed out (The Confession of God's Word) in order for you to get them to paint a picture for you. Pray, asking the Holy Spirit, "Give me a scripture…that you want me to crack." And then, you keep at it, over and over and over again, until you break it open, and you're able to drink of its sweet nectar!

God asked Joshua, "Do you want to know how to make it, where Moses failed?" And now God is asking you, "Do you want to know the secret to your future? This Book must never depart out of your mouth. You must meditate on it day and night, so that you'll *see yourself doing* according to all that's written therein; for then you…will make your way prosperous and then you…will have good success" (See Joshua 1:8).

Many believers visibly bristle when I talk about pursuing the Word of God with this much fervency. I often hear the following responses:

"Wow, you're so intense. Do you have to be so serious about this?"

"The Bible gives me good guidelines for living, but I don't think it has to completely consume my thinking."

"I already know the Word. But I also have a life. I'd have to be some kind of monk to do what you're talking about."

This is where many people unknowingly make a mistake; this is where the greatest failure of their life may be. If we think that we *know* a scripture—even one scripture—we must think again.

A person can memorize and quote thousands of scriptures. But that doesn't mean he *knows* any of them. We must go beyond "knowing it" mentally, and let it paint a picture *in our hearts.*

Many people who profess to be Christians "know" a lot of scriptures, but continue to live in sin. If we "know" a lot of scriptures, but we're not staying in them long enough for them to paint a picture, we begin to think that God's Word doesn't work. Then our perception becomes perverted, because our inside character is not keeping up with our outside intake of knowledge. To really *get the picture* within a scripture, we should choose to meditate on *one* scripture hundreds of times, instead of reading hundreds of scriptures one time!

If a person is living without pictures, it's because he is passing through what I like to call, "The Death Valley of Religion." Remember this: Religion is the death valley of your spiritual life. It's where you know things in your head, but cannot produce them in your life. Religion *downloads* the Word into your mind, but it doesn't *install* it into your heart. Unless it is installed into the hard-drive of your heart, it cannot produce.

> IT IS IMPOSSIBLE
> FOR GOD'S PROMISES
> TO EVER PRODUCE WITHOUT
> A HEALTHY INNER IMAGE.

That's the reason people can stand up and preach on love, yet come down from the pulpit and not believe anyone loves them. This is also the reason why someone can teach you about being a great husband, but when he goes home, he is anything *but* one himself. We must stand on God's promises, not just sit on His premises!

If you want a new future, God's Word must not depart out of your mouth. You meditate on it day and night, because it will paint you a picture of what God has *already* given you. You're not getting a picture of something new that's being created for you. It will be a picture of what's *already yours*.

When you see *the picture,* you will become tenacious and immovable in your faith. You won't have to beg for a miracle, and you won't have to deal with mental torment anymore. You will finally be free!

CHAPTER 5

What Are You Looking At?

People do not attract what they want; they attract what they *think*. Whatever you focus on grows. It becomes bigger in your mind and more influential in your actions and decision-making processes. Because I know this to be true, I have made it a daily discipline to ask myself this question: *"Have I been focusing on the problems, or have I been focusing on God?"*

IT IS IMPOSSIBLE TO ESCAPE THE HARVEST OF OUR MOST PRESENT THOUGHTS.

It is foolish to expect success in our lives if the majority of our thoughts focus on failure. Health will elude us if all we do is think about our aches, pains, and ailments. We will never experience prosperity if our thoughts are endlessly rehearsing our regrets, bitterness, or hopelessness over being impoverished. ***Every thought that you agree with becomes a powerful magnet, drawing into your life the manifested reality of the picture it holds.***

Usually, people's thoughts are focused on their desire to leave something, rather than to *move toward* something. For example, many people focus on wanting to lose weight: but they focus on *eliminating fat,* rather than on *moving toward being fit.* Their thoughts are focused on the fat, and yet they expect their bodies to move in the direction of being fit. It is impossible! Your body (and your life) will always go in the direction of your most dominant thoughts. Therefore, you must focus on where you want to go, ***not*** on what you'd like to leave behind.

2 Corinthians 4:18 tells us, "… we do not look at the things which are seen, but at the things which are not seen. For the things which are seen are temporary, but the things which are not seen are eternal."

You are doing one of two things at all times. You are either looking at the things that you can see, or you are looking at the things that you may not see yet, but know, from God's Word, to be true. You have to ask yourself in every situation, "Which one am I looking at? Am I looking at what I see, or am I looking at what I don't see?" For the things which are seen are temporary.

For example, one minute we can be saying, "I'm so hungry. I'm just so hungry. I'm really hungry," and the next minute, "Oh, I'm so full. I'm so full. I'm really full";—because natural situations are temporary.

I could say, "I've got a lot of money in the bank." Then, I write a check. "Now, I've got no money in the bank." Things that we see with our natural eye are very temporary.

So, in order to overcome the temporary, you look at the eternal. *"…we look not at the things which are seen, but at the things which are not seen.*

For the things which are seen are temporal, [they're subject to change] but the things that are not seen—[which is the Word of God]—these things are eternal" (2 Corinthians 4:18).

God's Word is eternal. It is the ever-unchanging truth of God. It is the *only* thing that will not change. Everything is going to come back to the Word of God.

Even in daily situations, I say to myself, "Now, why do you want to get depressed? Don't you realize that you've got to come back to where you are right now? Why do you want to go down? You just have to come back up again!"

So, the lowest I'm ever going to be is what I am right now; this is the worst you'll ever see me. I'm going *up* from here. I'll take a little step up and put my stake in the ground; and that's where I'll stay until I'm ready to take another step up. I'm not going backwards again.

"But don't you see all these horrible things that are going on?"

I didn't say I don't see them. I said I'm not *looking* at them. It's when you *look* at them that you get depressed. So, I'm not going to look at them.

"Aren't you just in denial?"

I'm not denying that those situations exist; but they are the *outside picture.* They are *a* truth. They are *temporary—subject to change, and not to be trusted.* As I spend more time focusing on the unseen eternal picture, the visible distractions will become *invisible* and *unimportant.*

What I choose to look at and focus upon is the picture of success and victory that the Word of God has painted inside of me. That picture is eternal, and *will not change.* It is *The Truth, and the only thought to be trusted.* When this is my focus, true change happens.

In Deuteronomy 30:15 and19, God gave us one of the keys of the kingdom. He said, *"See—see—see."* It begins with the word see. Now, I thought that was interesting. The word *see* begins the verse, because that's exactly what He wants us to focus on. He said, *"See, I have set before you..."*

Now, what most people see in life are the things that are set before them *on the outside;* and they're consistently making wrong decisions, based upon these temporal (temporary) conditions. They're choosing the wrong things. Remember:

YOUR CIRCUMSTANCES MUST NEVER DICTATE YOUR INNER IMAGE; IT IS YOUR INNER IMAGE THAT MUST DICTATE YOUR CIRCUMSTANCES!

God said, *"See, I have set before you life and death, blessing and cursing; but you choose life."* ***You must choose to see the new picture that the Word has painted on the inside, for it will bring you life!*** This is God's way, and it *will* work in your life!

Chapter 6

Your Future Is In Your Mouth

The business of renewing your mind and confessing God's Word is an *active* endeavor. You cannot just passively absorb Biblical principles by desire! You've got to be hungry for change in your life.

YOU ARE EITHER
A PRISONER TO YOUR PAST
OR A PIONEER OF YOUR FUTURE.

If you are a first generation Christian, you can consider yourself a pioneer, not only of your own future, but also of generations to come. Like pioneers of old, you are blazing a spiritual trail where no previous track was laid out. But you need not fear, for the compass of God's Word will never fail you. Choose to pay attention to the future–it's where you'll spend the rest of your life!

But, *how* do we do this? In Proverbs 4:20-23, the Bible tells us this:

> **My son, give attention to my words;**
> **Incline your ear to my sayings.**
> **Do not let them depart from your eyes;**
> **Keep them in the midst of your heart;**
> **For they are life to those who find them,**
> **And health to all their flesh.**
> **Keep your heart with all diligence;**
> **For out of it spring the issues of life.**

The *New Living Translation* gives us further insight:

> **Pay attention, my child, to what I say. Listen carefully.**
>
> **Don't lose sight of my words. Let them penetrate deep within your heart, for they bring life and radiant health to anyone who discovers their meaning.**

Above all else, guard your heart, for it affects everything you do.

Proverbs 3:1-4 says,

**My son, do not forget my law,
But let your heart keep my commands;
For length of days and long life
And peace they will add to you.
Let not mercy and truth forsake you;
Bind them around your neck,
Write them on the tablet of your heart,
And so find favor and high esteem
In the sight of God and man.**

Every time the devil attacks your mind with an oppressive thought, you stand at a fork in the road. Each time, you must make the choice either to believe and speak *the thought* or to believe and speak *the Word*. And each time, God's Word stands as a clear, immovable signpost, pointing the way to the path you should take; your task is simply to obey.

I call heaven and earth as witnesses today against you, that I have set before you life and death, blessing and cursing; *therefore choose life*, that both you and your descendants may live.

Deuteronomy 30:19-20

Paul understood that *active pursuit* of God's thoughts was the only way a person could truly be free. Philippians 3:13-14 reveals the passion of Paul's pursuit:

> **No, dear brothers and sisters, I am still not all I should be, but I am focusing all my energies on this one thing: Forgetting the past and looking forward to what lies ahead, I strain to reach the end of the race and receive the prize for which God, through Christ Jesus, is calling us up to heaven.**
>
> *Philippians 3:13-14 (NLT)*

Renewing your mind requires your participation. God can't do it for you; you must speak the Word for yourself. He has called *you* to be the architect of all your tomorrows—and to construct the future with the words of your mouth! I'd rather do the work of constructing my future, than to merely exist as a hostage to expectation.

Refuse to be a hope peddler, even to yourself. *Do what needs to be done* to create the future you desire! To create, God ***spoke.*** To create your future, you must do the same. Romans 10:8 *(NLT)* says, *"Salvation that comes from trusting Christ—which is the message we preach—is already within easy reach. In fact, the Scriptures say, 'The message is close at hand; it is on your lips and in your heart.'"* Paul is telling you that salvation—that is, deliverance, freedom, and victory in any arena of life—is within easy reach, if you are willing to open your mouth and call it in.

"Well, just exactly what should I be saying?"

Jesus made it quite clear where we would find the truth we must have in order to win in this life: *"Sanctify them by Your truth. Your word is truth"* (John 17:17). Consider David's declaration of the delivering power of God's Word to those who are committed to believing it, saying it, and doing it:

Happy are people of integrity, who follow the law of the LORD.

Happy are those who obey his decrees and search for him with all their hearts.

They do not compromise with evil, and they walk only in his paths.

You have charged us to keep your commandments carefully.

Oh, that my actions would consistently reflect your principles!

Then I will not be disgraced when I compare my life with your commands.

Psalm 119:1-6 (NLT)

MY OUTWARD ACTIONS ARE LITTLE MORE THAN A DISPLAY OF MY INNER CONVICTIONS.

Scripture is *completed by action*. Your first action step to freedom is renewing your mind and saying only what God says. Disappointment, depression, and mental torment are only the results of a person refusing to open his mouth and take action. This is illustrated clearly in God's conversation with Cain, in Genesis 4:6-7(NLT):

"Why are you so angry?" the LORD asked him. "Why do you look so dejected? You will be accepted if you respond in the right way. But if you refuse to respond correctly, then watch out! Sin is waiting to attack and destroy you, and you must subdue it."

If you don't keep your mind renewed, and your mouth full of God's Word, your old dead man will haunt and dominate you.

WE MUST NEVER GIVE LIFE TO WHAT GOD HAS PUT TO DEATH.

You need to keep the dead in its spiritual grave. How? Continual input of "living thoughts" (God's Word) will push out the dead thoughts. Continual speaking of The Answer will push out the problems.

> **The mouth of the righteous man utters wisdom, and his tongue speaks what is just. The law of his God is in his heart; his feet do not slip.**
>
> ***Psalm 37:30-31 (NIV)***

> **Do not snatch the word of truth from my mouth, for I have put my hope in your laws. I will always obey your law, for ever and ever. I will walk about in freedom, for I have sought out your precepts. I will speak of your statutes before kings and will not be put to shame.**
>
> ***Psalm 119:43-46 (NIV)***

> **Set a guard, O LORD, over my mouth; keep watch over the door of my lips. Do not incline my heart to any evil thing, to practice wicked works with men who work iniquity; and do not let me eat of their delicacies.**
>
> ***Psalm 141:3-4***

YOUR SPIRIT WILL PRODUCE THAT WHICH IT HEARS YOUR MOUTH SPEAK.

Proverbs 6:2 says, *"You are snared by the words of your mouth; you are taken by the words of your mouth."* Pay attention to your thoughts and your words throughout the day. When you notice a negative thought, replace it with God's thought. When you install God's thoughts into your mental hardware, they will erase all previously diseased or contaminated thoughts.

Here is an example of how I implemented these principles.

I knew that Philippians 4:6 said we should "take care for nothing." But, it seemed like everyone that I came into contact with was telling me to take care. In fact, it was always their parting remark, spoken almost like a blessing.

"It was nice to see you again —Take care!"

"Good talking to you—Take care!"

I knew that their motive was to simply wish me well, and that to them, "Take care" was an innocent, cordial remark. But, I also knew how prone I could be to actually getting into care and anxiety, and I didn't want others encouraging me to do so!

So, I had to tell the devil something. I said, "Devil, I'm going to tell you this right now. The next time someone says to me, 'Take care,' I will give you what God said about me taking care."

So, every time someone said, "Take care," I said, *"I don't care about anything, but in everything, by prayer and supplication with thanksgiving, I let my requests be made known to God. And the peace of God, which passes all understanding, shall keep my heart and mind in Christ Jesus. Finally, my brethren, whatsoever things are true, honest, just, pure, lovely, or of good report, if anything has any virtue or if anything has any praise, I think on these things"* (See Philippians 4:6-8).

Yes, I got more than a few surprised and shocked reactions! However, Satan no longer got my permission to come over and bring his demon-friend, Care, into the playground of my life!

Now, after awhile, I got a little more "sophisticated." Someone would say, "Take care," and I'd say, "Thank you very much." And *then*, I would turn my attention to the devil and say, "Okay, now I'm talking to you. I don't care about anything, but in everything by prayer and supplication with thanksgiving…"

This process went on for about a month; but after that, hardly anyone said, "Take care" to me. In the past twenty-five years, I've only been told to take care maybe half-a-dozen times! If you want to *stop* something, all you need to do is find out what to *start*. If you start saying God's Word, the mental torment will stop.

It may appear to you that I made a big deal over a "harmless comment." But you must examine *every* thought or comment, no matter how innocent it may seem. Ask the question: When held up to the truth of God's Word, does it stand? Remember Paul's admonitions:

> **Don't copy the behavior and customs of this world, but let God transform you into a new person by changing the way you think. Then you will know what God wants you to do, and you will know how good and pleasing and perfect his will really is.**
>
> ***Romans 12:2 (NLT)***
>
> **For though we live in the world, we do not wage war as the world does. The weapons we fight with are not the weapons of the world. On the contrary, they have divine power to demolish strongholds. We demolish arguments and every pretension that sets itself up against the**

knowledge of God, and we take captive every thought to make it obedient to Christ.

2 Corinthians 10:3-5 (NIV)

Friend, there is a great creative power in your words. If you want to create the victorious future that God has planned for you, make sure that you are speaking His Word!

Chapter 7

Be Responsive, Not Reactive

The real key to mind prosperity is getting out in front of the curve, instead of being behind it all the time. Don't just react to the things that the devil brings into your life. *Act*, before he ever shows up. Make the decision to be *responsive*, not *reactive*.

A PLAN OF ACTION IS WHAT PRECEDES A TRIUMPHANT FUTURE.

This means that *before* somebody ever tells me "Take care," I'm already saying, "I don't care about anything, but in everything, by prayer and supplication, with thanksgiving, I let my requests be made known to God." Now I'm fighting Satan *offensively*, instead of *defensively*.

So before guilt, shame, unbelief, condemnation, sickness, and all those destructive things can come to me, I've already spent time confessing what God said about them. ***I've already replaced the thought before it ever came.*** By the Word of God, I am now seeing into the spirit world, and I have my answers before the problems even arrive!

Before you ever hear the devil's objection, you must have already made your statement and given your judgment. Jesus said in John 7:24, *"Don't judge by mere appearance, but make a righteous judgment"* (author's paraphrase). The righteous judgment is *what God says*. Psalm 19:7-14 says that *God's Word* is God's righteous judgment. As you get out in front of the curve, it will change your life.

Perhaps you are saying, "That might work for you, but you just don't know what the devil is telling me."

Yes, certainly I do. He's telling you, "You're going to lose. Things aren't going to work out. Your marriage is failing. Your kids are rebellious and will destroy their lives and yours. Everything is horrible. Your friends are betraying you and things are bad. You're not going to have any money. You're going to grow up and get old, and no one's going to visit you."

"How did you know?!"

Because he says the same things to everyone! He doesn't change anything! Friend, remember this—life does not change for anyone. It's when *you* posture differently toward life that you get a different outcome than everyone else. The same things come to everyone! It's when *you* change that your circumstances change.

FREEDOM IS BIRTHED THE MOMENT I TAKE GOD AT HIS WORD.

If you have consistently meditated on the Word for any length of time, it will take quite a long time for torment to actually penetrate that barrier. You have built an almost unassailable wall around your mind with the Word of God. But once that torment has broken down the barrier that you have built, it will not want to let you go. However, it still amazes me how quickly torment will leave, the moment that you become *consistent* in the Word. It just cannot stay.

But you must become *steadfast and unwavering* in your meditation and confession of God's Word. It's not something that can come and go. To be effective, it has to become an everyday exercise.

Don't do anything by discipline. Do it by habit. It's what you do *consistently* that will determine the outcome of your life. In order to break free, God's Word must continually be in your mouth. If you're going to speak, say what God says; then watch your life for the inconsistencies of your actions and words. Remember this principle:

THE INSTRUCTION YOU FOLLOW WILL DETERMINE THE OUTCOME OF YOUR LIFE.

Follow the instruction of God's Word, and then *<u>you</u> will make your way prosperous and no man or devil in hell can stop you!*

Give yourself unreservedly to the meditation of

the Word of God. Ponder it and orally recite it, both day and night, until it paints a brilliantly clear picture within you. Then, refusing to look at what you see with your natural eyes, focus instead on what you see with your spiritual eyes. As you do, you will be able to laugh at the days ahead—for you will already know the inexpressible blessings that the future holds for you!

About The Author

A dynamic speaker and author, Dr. Robb D. Thompson, America's Leading Expert On Personal Excellence, is recognized as an exceptionally skilled relational and leadership strategist. He is dedicated to helping people excel and maximize their full potential.

Pragmatic and dynamic, he shares principles, concepts and ideas that are applicable and effective to everyone using the following tools:

- *Speaker*. Travels more than 4 million miles around the globe for conferences, seminars, and workshops speaking to over 5,000 audiences in 5 different continents in 20 countries on topics such as leadership, success, and relationships.
- *Author*. Currently authored more than eighteen compelling books and numerous magazine articles. Also has created numerous audio and video resources.

- ***Robb Thompson International, Inc.***
  President & Founder. Dedicated to helping people excel in life–corporate, Governmental, and future leaders across the world. (www.robbthompson.com)
- ***The Gabriel Call*** – Vice Chairman.
  A program dedicated to raising up and training entrepreneurs around the world
- ***Family Harvest Church***
  Founder and Senior Pastor
- ***Excellence In Ministry International***
  President and Founder. A global ministerial association of pragmatic leaders
- ***International College of Excellence***
  President and Founder.
- ***Winning In Life*** – Host. Weekly television show viewed by millions in the United States and around the world.

Books by Robb Thompson

Start pressing towards excellence and a higher quality of life! Using the integrated tools and resources developed by Robb Thompson, you will take control of every facet of your life–achieve optimum financial status, live every day with passion, and master essential life principles. Make a commitment today to hold yourself accountable for your personal growth

<u>Other Books By Robb Thompson</u>

The Ten Critical Laws of Relationship
Victory Over Fear
You Are Healed
Marriage From God's Perspective
The Great Exchange
Winning the Heart of God
Shattered Dreams
Give Up Worry Forever

Books To Be Released Soon!

Your Passport To Promotion:
*11 Principles To Get Ahead In Your Career
And Get The Promotion You Deserve*

Promotion must be earned; it is not a result of your existence. Robb Thompson challenges you to change, inspires you to grow, and equips you to maximize your career performance. The principles outlined in this book are the tools needed to see your highest aspirations fulfilled in today's job market and business world.

Winning In Life Principles

Winning In Life Principles is a collection of some of the most powerful statements spoken and written by author and speaker, Robb Thompson. It is truly a priceless gift of aphorisms, wisdom, and principles from America's leading expert on personal Excellence.

For a complete listing of additional
products by Robb Thompson, please call:

1-877-WIN-LIFE

(1-877-946-5433)

You can also visit us on the web at:

www.winninginlife.org

To contact Robb Thompson, please write:

Robb Thompson

P. O. Box 558009

Chicago, Illinois 60655

***Please include your prayer requests
and comments when you write.***

Also please visit our site at:

www.robbthompson.com